The Origin of Love

The Origin of Love

On the Beauty of Compassion

Ryuho Okawa

Lantern Books • New York

A Division of Booklight Inc.

Lantern Books
A Division of Booklight Inc.
Lantern Books
128 Second Place
Brooklyn, NY 11231
www.lanternbooks.com

Printed in the United States of America

ISBN: 978-1-59056-313-7
Earlier edition appeared under ISBN: 1-59056-052-3

Table of Contents

Preface

Like my previous book, *The Starting Point of Happiness*, this book was also written with the aim of introducing the basic teachings of Happy Science, which I founded, to a wider audience.

Love is the first of the "principles of happiness," which I have named "the Noble Fourfold Path," after Shakyamuni Buddha's Noble Eightfold Path. The very essence of love is to be found in the beauty of compassion, which is evident throughout this book.

The first chapter was released as a booklet written for Happy Science members, the second chapter is a lecture I gave at a seminar which used Chapter One as the text. Chapters Three to Eight were written to be released as our monthly magazines. I have decided to make the basic teachings of our organization public so that those who wish may join.

Ryuho Okawa
Founder and CEO
Happy Science Group
August 2001

Chapter One

The Origin of Love

1. The Significance of Love

I would like to talk about love. Love has been described in many different ways by many different people. Most of you have probably wondered from time to time what true love is. At this very moment, some of you may be suffering on account of love, and others of you may feel surrounded by it. For a long time I, too, have given this much thought and now I would like to share my current thinking about love with you, my interim report on love.

First of all, I would like to define love in the following way. The essence of love is to be found in the soul's desire to be reunited with God from whom we originated. As we live our individual lives with our different personalities, we remember the ultimate parent and wish to go back to the bosom, to return to the one original source. This is the basis of love.

It is vital to accept the idea that we all originate from one being. The truth is that all human beings, as well as plants and animals, originate from one single source. In this respect, we can say that love is a feeling of oneness with others. Love is based on the understanding that you and others are not separate but essentially one, and loving others is exactly the same as loving yourself. Similarly, when you love others, it means that you love God Himself.

The significance of love is to be found in the fact that we who have separated call out to each other, trying to reunite and create greater happiness together. This is not simply an abstract idea. Why do a man and a woman try and unite? Because they have a natural desire to help each other improve.

Human beings could not improve themselves if no one else existed. Imagine, for instance, you were shipwrecked and landed on a desert island like Robinson Crusoe. Even if you somehow managed to survive, how could you find any motivation to become a better person? It is only in relation to others that you are able to confirm whether or not you are developing spiritually.

We could not assess ourselves if we were completely alone. The existence of other people is the basis for our judgments of ourselves. By observing the reactions of others, sensing how they look at us and treat us, we come to know what is necessary to refine our souls further. The very presence of other people is in itself love. Without others, we cannot improve or make progress, nor can we experience true happiness, although it is also the case that we have worldly desires and create suffering through our relationships with others.

2. The Beginning of Love

Now let us consider the beginning of love. Why do human beings have the urge to love one another? Why would a man and a woman wish to join together? Why would a husband and wife intend to live together for the rest of their lives? Why does the parent–child relationship exist and how can this relationship be sustained for many years?

Take, for example, the affection in a parent–child relationship. Parents love their children; but is it simply because they have given birth to them? Theoretically it would be possible for mothers to forget their offspring as soon as they had given birth, as in the case with certain animals. However, we are happy to have a baby of our own, and feel joy through mutual learning and sharing of experiences in the process of raising children.

Why is this? Have parents been given any instructions they should feel this way? Do parents love their children because they have learned somewhere about the wonder of loving their offspring? Do children love their parents because they have been taught to? What about a husband and wife? Does a husband love his wife because someone has convinced him it is a good thing to do so? Does a wife love her husband because she has been told she should? Why do people fall in love?

Pondering these questions, I have come to the conclusion that love has a beginning, and it is the source of energy that flows through human life. I believe that this fundamental energy is love; it is the power to nurture each other, and help one another improve.

Both this world and the next are overflowing with the energy of love. Everything that comprises our diet is also made of this energy. Why do crops and vegetables become fuel for our physical bodies? They, too, are the very manifestation of the energy of love. Why is an apple so tasty? Why are tomatoes and cabbages edible? When we think in this way, we can see all the energy we are given in the course of a life on Earth is nothing less than the energy of love from others.

Love is the feeling of wanting to be of service to others; love is not for your own sake. After all, plants and animals also have this impulse. They, too, are made of the energy of love. What is more, this energy is not only confined to this world; the same energy also runs through the spirit world. It is the power that grants eternal life to human beings, showering on us from afar, from beyond the universe.

Through reading the books of the Truth you may have learned that human beings are blessed with eternal life. But what does this mean? How is it possible that life is eternal? In this world, no machine works forever; although this is possible in theory, in practice we cannot manufacture a machine like this. But why does the soul live eternally? Why does it never wear out or fade away?

The power that nurtures this everlasting life is the power of God's love. The very fact that energy lives forever is proof that the energy of love is being showered upon us eternally. I believe that love has its source in the fact that all beings, human and non-human, have eternal life. For life to be eternal, there must be a permanent supply of energy, the power of God, that allows us to live eternally. This is the very beginning of love.

3. What Obstructs Love

What, then, are the obstructions to love? What tries to stop the flow of love? Here I would like to explore some answers to these questions. I have just explained that the beginning of love is to be found in the fact that we have eternal life. I have also explained that love is the power to nurture one another, without differentiating between the self and others. Following on from this, I can say that an obstacle to love is anything that goes against these two ideas.

What contradicts these two ideas? First is a mindset which denies that human beings have eternal life. This denial obstructs the flow of love because the idea that human beings live only one life gives rise to egotism. The belief that we will end up as dust and ashes after some decades of earthly life causes us to become self-centered, asserting our egos. This self-centered view distinguishes the self from others, and as a result, brings pain and sorrow.

People try to control others and rule over them as if they were the masters of slaves to satisfy their own desires. Why do people speak ill of others? Probably because they feel unable to control others, unable to make them think and behave as they would like. When you complain about someone, it is often because you have failed to make that person think or feel in the way you wanted them to.

All negative emotions such as dissatisfaction, worry, anger and jealousy have their roots in the belief that human life is limited to this world. So to awaken to true love, free of any obstructions, it is necessary first of all to know that life is eternal.

Another aspect of love we need to know about is the power to help one another to grow spiritually. What is this power, and what brings about spiritual improvement? The power to improve one another is in fact an attitude of giving to one another and a wish to benefit others. It is the opposite of trying to bring others down in the hope of raising one's own standing. Only when we direct love to each other will a wonderful world unfold before us.

Imagine two women, A and B. A is proud because her clothes are beautiful and is boasting about them. On the other hand, B insists that her clothes are much more beautiful. Let us assume that, actually, both are wearing beautiful clothes. Compare this situation to one where, instead, each admires the other's clothes. The world that would emerge would be completely different.

No matter how much you admire your own clothes, you will not be able to feel true delight, like the luster of a pearl; your joy will soon fade. On the other hand, when you honestly admire another's clothes you will experience real pleasure, and so will the other person. If the other person admires your clothes in turn, not only will you feel pleasure, the other person will as well. This is the art of loving—a technique for happiness—and it is important to make good use of this method.

As this example shows, the second obstruction to love is a mindset that separates the self from others, trapping the self in a whirlpool of loneliness. To be free of this obstruction, it is important always to have a willingness to make others happy. If you have this wish, you too will be given joy and happiness by many. In the end, jealousy, fear, suspicion, abuse, complaints, pain and sorrow all come to the fore because we lock ourselves in a cage of sorrow, a lonely world where people never give to each other.

So, we should ask ourselves every day: "What can I give others today? What can I say, or how can I offer a smile? How will I express compassion when I meet others?" If society was filled with people with this attitude, this would be enough to transform this Earth into an ideal world. Creating an ideal society is not so difficult. If each person is determined to bring joy to others and make them happy, this is sufficient. Herein lies the first step to creating an ideal world. This is something we always need to remember.

4. Transcending Good and Evil

Now I would like to discuss the theme of good and evil in relation to love. The dualism of good and evil has long been an important topic, not least of all in Christianity. People have long debated why evil exists in this world if God, the supreme power and the source of all good, is all-powerful. They have also argued about why an archangel went to hell and whether this was part of God's plan or an accident.

The truth is beyond human understanding, but one thing I can say is that the world is not simply divided into two realms, heaven and hell. In the course of your life on Earth, you will find that everyone has different opinions. Suppose there were ten people, and one of them had an idea that was completely different from the ideas of the rest and found it difficult to make the others understand his or her thinking. It is conceivable that in this situation, the person would feel disconnected from the group. This is the source that gives rise to evil.

Even if one person has a different opinion from the others, it does not mean that his or her idea is wrong; it simply means that others cannot understand it, and that person has failed to make others understand. From this we can say that the origin of evil is closely connected to an inability to understand others, or convince them of something.

If you could understand everyone in this world, you would be able to forgive them all. To understand all would lead you to forgive all. It is because you cannot understand others that you regard them as enemies and begin to criticize. Discontent and complaints also arise when you feel you are not being understood. Why can others not understand you? The reason is that you have been unable to communicate your ideas.

Evil comes into being because people cannot read each other's minds. Before we are born in this world, the minds of others are as transparent as glass, so we can understand their thoughts, but once we live in this world in a physical body, we can no longer read people's minds. People do not know exactly what others are thinking and this gives rise to many problems.

If everyone's thoughts were transparent, basically evil would not arise. However, because people cannot read the minds of others, they are unable to understand someone else's thinking or explain their own ideas successfully, so negative feelings come into being. On Earth, we each live in a physical body which is a vehicle for the soul's development but this also becomes an obstacle to mutual understanding.

What, then, can we do to overcome this problem? When we cannot understand another person, what should we do? One way to solve this is to align ourselves with the mind of a third person, one who reflects the will of God. If this person is able to teach God's words, it is important that each individual attunes his or her mind and spiritual vibration to that teaching. By doing this, we will be able to build a common basis for mutual understanding and share our views of life with one another. For this reason, it is necessary to support the transmission of God's will.

Acquiring knowledge of the Truth is the way to transcend good and evil. We can go beyond good and evil through understanding the Truth because this knowledge serves to remove the obstacles to an understanding of others. By studying and conveying the Truth, we will be able to break through any walls that separate the self from others and prevent mutual understanding. Knowledge of the Truth is the power that enables us to transcend good and evil. We should be aware of how great a power this is.

5. The Origin of Love

I have talked about love from several different angles; lastly, I would like to discuss the origin of love. The basis of love is humility. Love does not have any arrogance or self-centered attitudes, for instance, "because I am better than anyone else, it is I who will lead people." Love embodies selflessness and the wish to be of service, without expecting anything in return. The purer our wish and our motivation, the more beautiful the love we give.

Love evolves in the process of pursuing beauty. Love reflects how beautifully your soul is giving out light. The beautiful light of the soul is the origin of love. Be careful not to mistake the starting point. We need to think about what is necessary so that our souls give out the most beautiful light.

Why does a diamond shine so beautifully? Because each of its facets is well balanced. If the form of a diamond is irregular, like a pomegranate that has cracked open, this will create shadows across light and it is no longer be considered beautiful. A diamond is beautiful as a result of the balance of its shape.

Similarly, it is important that our souls emit a well-balanced light. In other words, we need to develop and manifest every aspect of God's character. God is love, knowledge, courage, light, wisdom, justice and also compassion. Each of these qualities that God embodies shines brilliantly, like the facet of a diamond. Eternal evolution in the attempt to acquire all these qualities is the path that will bring about the soul's development.

Love begins from the endeavor to create a beautiful brilliance of soul. To create this brilliance, we need to acquire as many of God's qualities as possible, find these qualities within ourselves and refine them so that they shine forth. It is also important that each of these qualities has the beauty of harmony and balance.

Here lies our goal, the goal of human life, which is to attempt to incorporate as much of God's nature as possible, to balance the different aspects and allow them to shine brilliantly. Do not be satisfied with small achievements. Do not focus on just one facet of God. God embodies many characteristics, so strive to master them all, and in the process, aim to create harmony in everything. Here is the path to eternal evolution; it is the origin of love, the starting point of the journey toward love, because love is the very manifestation of God, the most beautiful, brilliant diamond.

Chapter Two

To Make Your Soul Shine Beautifully:

A Lecture on "The Origin of Love"

1. The Definition of Love

In this chapter, I would like to continue to expand on the ideas in Chapter One. Although from ancient times love has been described in many different ways, there is no fixed definition of love. Love and hate arise constantly among the six billion people living on Earth, and it is difficult for us to see what true love that accords with God's will is. Perhaps you are now studying the teachings of love in a theoretical way; but how to actually practice love in everyday life and apply it to human relationships is a never-ending challenge.

I would like to start by talking about the meaning of love. Among the many teachings of Happy Science, special emphasis is placed on the theme of love. This is because understanding love was the first gateway through which I entered the path of enlightenment. Soon after I came into contact with the spirit world, I was given a key phrase: "love, nurture and forgive others." It was predicted that these words would be the core of a philosophy I would later teach. However, the time was not yet ripe, so I continued to reflect on these words, wondering how I could put them into practice and develop them further as teachings.

As I continued to contemplate these words, the theory of the developmental stages of love gradually evolved in my mind. I contemplated the meaning of loving, nurturing, forgiving—thinking about each word separately, and the relationship between them. Then I found there were different levels in love. I also came to discover another form of love higher than forgiving, which I named the "incarnation of love." I was convinced that there was a level of love beyond the human sphere.

As I said at the beginning of this chapter, the subject of love raises as many questions as there are different people and situations, so it would take a very long time to give answers to cover every eventuality in human relationships. This is why I would like to discuss love in a more general way, based on my present ideas.

To begin with, I would like to define love in the following way. Every human being was originally a part of God, the supreme consciousness. Then we separated from Him to become individual beings with different personalities. As we lead our individual lives, there are moments when we remember the ultimate parent and want to return to our source. This feeling is the basis of love.

If you explore deeply, you will surely find memories of the source within you. Why else do you have an urge to love others? Why do you accept without question that it is wonderful to love? If you reflect in the depths of your heart, you will recall feelings from a distant past. Love is the power of attracting and joining with one another. This power takes us back to the far distant past and reminds us of memories that are familiar to us.

We do not love others or continue to give love simply because we have been taught to. Deep down, we are all strongly attracted to the idea of loving others. Once the veil that covers the true self has been removed, we can feel how marvelous it truly is to love.

If the heart were a wasteland where we could find only stones and rubble no matter how deeply we dug, then even if we were to sow many seeds in its ground, there would never be any harvest. But actually, when we sow the seeds of love in our hearts, they sprout, grow and bear fruit, which shows that the soil in our hearts is far from barren. There may be rubble or weeds on the surface but once we dig the ground, we will find a rich soil ready to accept the seeds of love. As if it has been waiting for these seeds, the soil provides abundant energy to nurture them.

Explore and dig deep within yourself if you want to check and see whether what I have said is true, that all human beings originate from the one source. Then you will be able to find out whether you have a desire to love others because you have been taught or forced to, or whether this feeling comes naturally from the depths of your own heart.

The basis of love is the idea that the self is not separate from others and that originally we were one, so that loving others is synonymous with loving yourself and loving God. There are no limits to the depth at which you can understand this, although at present this is still probably no more than just a theory to you. Nevertheless, the first step is to know it intellectually.

2. The Existence of Others

Why do a man and a woman wish to join together? The reason must be they expect they can help each other improve through being together. If there is no one else around, you cannot refine your soul.

In Chapter One, I talked about Robinson Crusoe. Have you ever thought about how wonderful it is that other people exist? When you come into contact with many people, at times you may feel hurt, upset or even offended. You may sometimes feel resentful about the way people see you in relation to others. Perhaps some people see themselves as autonomous beings, never affected by comparisons with others.

Actually, the fact that others exist is, in itself, a source of happiness. If you were leading an isolated life like Robinson Crusoe you could not ever savor real happiness. You need to realize how much of a positive influence other people have on your life. As a result of the reactions of others, the way they speak to you, look at you, and how they behave toward you, you experience happiness and feel your life is worth living. It is important to be aware that without others, you could not expect to make progress, refine your character or feel happiness.

This being so, even if you are feeling hurt or complain that you have dropped in another's estimation you need to accept your present situation with a big heart, and try to learn the lesson so that you can continue to develop. Those who cannot adopt this attitude are still a long way from enlightenment. The truth is that someone who you feel has hurt you is in essence connected to the very core of your soul, and that person is no one other than yourself.

We should aim to achieve a state of mind where we can experience the happiness of others as if it were our own; in actual fact, what we perceive as others is only an illusion created by our own eyes. From the viewpoint of God, the crowd of people in this world looks like a gathering of children of light, each radiating light like a chandelier. Every single person is a child of light in the eyes of God. Each person's light is of a different intensity, some stronger and some fainter; together they create a beautiful picture.

It is human nature to judge others by their appearance. By looking at other people's hair, eyes, noses, mouths, hands, legs and bodies, we feel that we are separate beings and that other people's happiness is of no importance to us unless it benefits us in some way. However, from the viewpoint of God, each of us shines in a multitude of colors, like the light of a chandelier. No matter which light is brighter, light is light and it is the source of joy.

3. Love—the Source of Energy

Here I would like to talk about the beginning of love. There is a natural desire for a parent and child or a man and woman to feel united. Most animals also instinctively take care of their young. In Chapter One, I asked the following set of questions: Do you think that you love your parents or children just because you have been taught that love is wonderful? Does a husband love his wife because he has been taught it is a good thing to do so? Does a wife love her husband because someone told her she should love him? Why do young people fall in love when they reach adolescence?

After contemplating such questions, I concluded that love has a beginning. It can be traced back to the source of energy that flows through human life. This fundamental energy is love. Love is the power to nurture and help one another improve.

We tend to be concerned only with human beings and think of love as existing only between people. However, we should sometimes look around and be aware of the love that sustains our lives. When we find how much love we have been given, we need to feel grateful. Take, for example, the love that is in our food. How much gratitude have you felt for what you eat? It is shameful not to feel any gratitude for the energy given to us by our food.

How many people feel thankful for vegetables, rice or wheat? How grateful are we for water and all the natural resources available for us? Have they ever expected anything in return from us? They are simply giving, without expectation of any reward. Human beings are said to be the lords of creation, and in the course of our lives, we tend to focus on how much we are being given, but have little interest in giving our love to others. We need to reflect deeply on this fact.

Let me focus on food. Why is an apple delicious? Why are tomatoes and cabbages good to eat? If we ate food only for the sake of fueling our physical bodies, it would not need to be tasty. The fact that the food we eat also tastes good is a manifestation of love.

Love is not for oneself; it is a wish to serve others. Plants and animals have the same wish and they are also expressions of the energy of love. We must sometimes look at our state and be aware that we are constantly provided with the energy and the environment to be able to live and develop.

Despite this fact, we are easily swayed by the opinions of others, and create suffering when we are dissatisfied with their assessments. What is worse, not only do we become trapped in suffering, but we also spread our affliction around us and have a negative influence on others. We sometimes need to reflect deeply, repent and correct our attitudes. It is important to realize how small we are, and spend some time looking at ourselves before God.

When we become aware of the energy of love that surrounds us, we come to understand the essence of the energy that runs through the spiritual world. It is a power that comes from far away, from beyond the universe, and gives eternal life to each and every human being.

As I said in Chapter One, human beings have eternal life. In contrast, there is no machine that can function forever. Although we live in an age of technological advances that produce a wide variety of machines, human beings have never created a machine that can remain in perpetual motion, nor will we ever be able to invent one in the future. But human souls live in a world of continual energy, which neither increases nor diminishes, and they never cease moving nor do they run out of energy.

If we were merely machines, it would not be surprising if our life force faded and eventually disappeared in the process of numerous reincarnations. However in reality, souls live forever. We are given energy that never lessens, allowing us eternal life. We have to give more thought to this mystical truth. The energy that nurtures eternal life is the power of love that comes from God. The fact that energy lives forever is proof that we are continually being provided with the abundant and inexhaustible energy of love.

The beginning of love is to be found in the fact that both humans and other living beings have eternal life. Life can be sustained eternally only if there is a perpetual supply of energy. I believe that love originates from the infinite energy of God that sustains our life eternally.

We are given love and eternal life. We need to realize that the very fact we are granted eternal life is the manifestation of God's love. God just gives infinitely, without expecting anything in return. If God's love were conditional and limited, it would not be surprising if we were to lose our lives the moment we went against His will. However, no matter what kind of life people lead, even if they curse God, everyone is equally promised eternal life. How do you understand this fact?

God allows the rain to fall on the good and the evil alike. It is an undeniable fact that no matter whether you are good or evil, whether you live in accordance with God's will or not, He continues to furnish you with eternal life. That is the nature of the ultimate love, infinite love. Only when you realize that you are continuously receiving this great love will you awaken to your true mission.

4. The Obstacles to Love

I stated earlier that the beginning of love is to be found in the eternal nature of life and that love is the energy with which we nurture one another, without distinction between the self and others. As I concluded in the previous chapter, an obstacle to love must then be any idea that contradicts these principles.

As I noted in Chapter One, denying that human life is eternal obstructs the great love of God, and gives rise to egotism. This denial leads to self-centeredness and the belief that we are separate and unconnected to others. As a result, we harm each other, and cause one another sorrow. We sometimes even attempt to dominate others and control them to satisfy our own desires.

Why do you speak ill of others? Probably because you cannot make them act as you would like them to. In the same way, if you complain about someone, it is probably because you feel unable to control what that person is thinking or feeling. Complaints, worry, anger, jealousy, in fact all negative emotions are against love, because these feelings originate from the idea that human life is limited. To be free of all obstacles to love and to awaken to true love, it is essential to believe that life is eternal.

Another aspect of love that I described is the power to help one another to grow spiritually. It is the power to give to one another, trying to act for the benefit of others instead of putting them down to raise our own standing. Only through giving love to one another can we create a wonderful world.

To explain this in a more understandable way, in Chapter One I used the example of two women who are beautifully dressed.

By expressing admiration for the clothes of the other, smiles and happiness will spread and increase, and the joy will last for a long time. This is one technique for attaining love and happiness, and it is important to learn this method and put it into practice.

So the second obstacle to love is the idea that you are separate from others, which causes you to remain locked in your own world. To overcome this obstacle you need to try to bring others happiness, then you too will receive joy and happiness. If you experience negative emotions and create suffering, it is because you have locked yourself into a lonely world, where you do not give.

This is why it is important to resolve to give love to others every day. Visualize yourself speaking compassionately, smiling, being thoughtful with others. When this world is full of people with this sort of attitude, an ideal world will be realized on Earth. Difficult theories are not necessary in creating an ideal world. All we need is to wish for other people's happiness and the actual practice of giving love. Always remember that these are the first steps to creating an ideal world.

5. The Dualism of Good and Evil

In discussing love, I must speak of an important issue, the dualism of good and evil; it is an eternal theme that always needs to be explored. Why does evil exist in this world and how should we view good and evil? If good and evil are completely contradictory, how should love respond to evil? In discussing love, we need to ponder these questions.

As I explained in the previous chapter, the world cannot simply be divided into two opposing realms, heaven and hell, and it is possible for us at least to understand the origin of good and evil. The reasons evil comes into being are to be found in daily life. As there are so many people and each one has different ideas, conflicting opinions naturally arise. The ability to understand others and make oneself understood is closely connected to the reasons that good and evil arise.

If you could understand everyone, you would forgive everyone, because understanding all would lead you to forgive all. As I said earlier, when we are born into this world and live in a physical body, we can no longer read other people's thoughts. This obstructs mutual understanding and causes negative feelings to arise.

How should we solve this problem? The solution is for each person to attune their thoughts to the same perspective, namely that of someone who can reflect the will of God, the supreme consciousness. If there is someone who can give God's teachings, it is necessary to attune our minds to the teachings of that person, which means living in accordance with the Laws of Truth.

If we all have a different sense of values and a different way of thinking and consequently are unable to understand one another, then why not establish a common basis for communication? This common basis must have its source in God; this means in the Laws of Truth. Even if we cannot read one another's thoughts, we can still communicate by valuing the Truth and adopting it. This is the reason many Angels of Light have incarnated on Earth as representatives of God, to convey His teachings repeatedly through different times and regions.

Here we can see the reason for teaching the Laws—to bring separate souls together and unite them. The Laws of Truth are given on Earth to teach us: "Take the Truth as the set of principles by which to live your life and learn the Truth as nourishment for your soul."

When we dwell in physical bodies, we cannot see into others' minds and that is the reason evil has come into being. However, we cannot say that God has made a mistake. Because human beings are far from perfect and unable to read one another's thoughts, we have been given God's teachings and His encouragement to live in accordance with the Truth. By trying to practice the Truth, we become able to know each other's thoughts in the same way as we are able to see through glass. On condition that we try to attune our hearts to the Truth, we are allowed to live individual lives with our own free will.

Acquiring knowledge of the Truth is the way to transcend good and evil. With the knowledge of the Truth we will be able to break through the walls that prevent mutual understanding and separate us from others. We can surmount these walls by studying and conveying the Truth to others. We have to break down the walls that block us off from others, and by attuning ourselves to the Truth, become connected with others. On Earth, we live and think as completely separate individuals, but we have to unite in the bonds of the Truth. This is the essence of faith. The knowledge of the Truth is a great power that enables us to transcend good and evil.

6. The Brilliance of the Soul

I have looked at love from a number of different angles. Lastly, I would like to talk about the origin of love. As I said in Chapter One, the basis of love is humility. Love is never compatible with arrogance, complacency or self-importance. It embodies selflessness and a willingness to be of service to others, without expecting any reward. The purer your wish to serve and the purer your motives for action, the more beautiful the love that you will give.

That leads me to the subject of love and beauty. Love evolves in the pursuit of beauty; it manifests in the beauty of the soul's light. In fact, the origin of love is the beautiful light of the soul. Since this is the case, do not misunderstand the starting point; you always need to consider what you can do so that your soul will give out the most beautiful light imaginable.

Why does a diamond shine so beautifully? The reason is that it has been cut and faceted in a shape that is regular and balanced. Similarly, it is important that your soul is well balanced, and that each facet gives out a brilliant light. What does it mean, to be well balanced? It means refining your soul so that it expresses the qualities of goodness that God embodies. God embodies so many qualities, including love, knowledge, courage, light, wisdom, justice, compassion, kindness and power. Each of these qualities shines brilliantly, like the planes of a diamond. By making an effort to assimilate all these qualities, you will be able to continue evolving eternally.

The starting point of love is the endeavor to increase the beauty of the inner light that a soul gives out. To increase the beauty of the soul, we need to assimilate as many of the qualities of God as possible. We need to find them within ourselves and refine them. It is also important that these qualities together create the beauty of harmony and balance. To attain this goal, what do we need to do? Here is the reason we learn the Truth, to transform it into strength, courage and nourishment for the soul.

To create the beauty of harmony and balance, do not hesitate to learn the Truth. Do not place limits on yourself, by creating boundaries. You need to make a constant effort. It is important to try to acquire as many of the qualities of God as possible, balance them and allow them to shine beautifully. God has such a vast array of attributes—strive to master them all, and in the process, aim to create a wonderful harmony of all the good qualities you have acquired. This is the path of eternal evolution.

Here is the origin of love, the starting point of the journey toward love, because love is the very being of God Himself, the most beautiful diamond. God is the ultimate manifestation of love, a diamond that gives out the most brilliant light called Truth. If you are attracted and moved by the beauty of this light, continue to advance steadily toward it without stopping, and create that same beauty within yourself. In this way, knowledge and love are united.

Chapter Three

The True Nature of Prayer

1. What Is Prayer?

I would like to talk about prayer. To pray means to conduct ourselves correctly before God and express our wishes. There are two questions that arise in relation to this: What is the significance of the act of conducting ourselves correctly before God and are there any restrictions on the content or nature of a prayer? These are the two issues that we need to examine.

First, let us think about what it means to conduct ourselves correctly before God. For this, there are three requirements. The first is humility. Without humility, we cannot present ourselves correctly to God. So when we pray, it is important that we conduct ourselves humbly and courteously.

The second requirement is to purify the mind, or remove any stains from the mind by reflecting on the dirt that is covering it, and if we have acted wrongly, to admit our mistakes and repent them. So the act of praying should be accompanied by purification of the mind.

Not only when we pray to God do we need to conduct ourselves correctly; when we meet someone we respect, we cannot help but act appropriately. We become concerned about what we are wearing, our appearance, our behavior and the expression on our face, and we even worry about what is in our minds. Originally, however, it is in relation to faith we need to feel this kind of concern.

Unless we purify our minds—in other words empty our minds and remove all worldly vibrations—we will not be able to restore a peaceful enough state of mind to be able to present ourselves to God. This is the reason we need to purify ourselves, and reflect on our thoughts and deeds, repenting our mistakes before we pray.

The third requirement is to know that the relationship between God and human beings is not a give-and-take relationship; it is not like a contract. In a business contract, for instance, there is a transaction, "I will give you this so you will give me that," but we cannot establish this kind of relationship with God. We need to acknowledge that there is a distinct difference between God and human beings.

In the case of office work, when a subordinate makes a proposal to a manager, it is the manager who decides whether the proposal should be taken up or if it needs any modification. Similarly, when a person prays to God, it is up to Heaven to determine what the outcome of a prayer will be. We need to accept this difference in standing and understand that God has the authority to judge whether or not our wishes will be realized.

This leads to the next question about the nature and content of a prayer. The content of a prayer must be appropriate in the light of God's will. If the content is inappropriate from the perspective of the Truth, and goes in an opposite direction to God, there is a strong possibility that the prayer will not be realized. So we always need to make sure that our prayers fulfill this requirement.

2. God and Human Beings

The act of praying is of great significance—it reminds us of the distinct difference between God and human beings. Around Shinto shrines, for example, there are usually extensive precincts and on reaching the front of a shrine, people often become aware of how tiny human beings really are. The same is true at Buddhist temples. When we stand before a huge statue of Buddha, we realize how small we are. In Christian churches too, when we kneel in prayer, we become very aware that we are tiny.

Prayer actually provides us with the opportunity to contemplate the difference that exists between God and human beings. It also gives us a way of reducing the distance and establishing contact with God. When we pray, we wonder whether or not our prayer reaches God. Actually, as long as we "dial" the correct "number," it is possible to contact the beings in the heavenly world; it is as if we were making a phone call. "Dialing the correct number" is closely related to our attitude to prayer, which I described earlier. If we maintain a correct approach and carefully consider the contents of our prayer, it will surely reach the heavenly world.

In the novel *Silence,* written by popular Japanese novelist Shusaku Endo (1923–1996), there is a description of the suffering of a missionary who has come to Japan. The missionary asks God why He does not answer his prayers and why He keeps silent.

However, God is not silent but rather eloquent. "God" here refers to the high spirits in the heavenly world. They hear my thoughts accurately, and if necessary, give me all sorts of advice. The reality is that the high spirits are by no means silent. They are anxious to inspire people on Earth because they are filled with love.

Love means having a giving heart, and high spirits want to give human beings what they hope for. Since the high spirits are full of love, we can be confident that there will always be some kind of answer to our prayers. Through prayer, we are given the chance to have access to heaven.

3. The Existence of High Spirits

When praying, we need to give some thought to the existence of high spirits. You can learn these things through my books on the Truth. It is important to know about high spirits and how to contact them.

High spirits are by their very nature unable to leave people alone; they cannot hold back from helping. Spirits in the spirit world hear the words of our prayers and if the nature of the prayer is appropriate in the light of God's will, the high spirits are willing to help us in some way. As a result, our prayers will be realized in the long term.

However, it is important that we do not become attached to our prayers. Once we have calmed our mind and said a prayer serenely in a correct manner, we should let it go and go on with our daily life with a calm mind. Our prayer will be realized at the appropriate time, and if it is not in accordance with the will of the high spirits, it will eventually disappear from our mind. The following examples will explain what I mean.

Suppose you have a strong wish to be promoted by your company and you pray for this. Then two months later, you are offered a very good job at another company, and so you change jobs. In this case, your prayer to be promoted was not realized but instead something unexpected happened to fulfill your wish. Or suppose you pray that you will marry a certain person. However, if that person is not a truly good partner for you, your feelings for that person will eventually disappear and you will be attracted to someone else.

It is important that we leave judgment to the high spirits. If we wish for something too strongly with our human minds, and if the wish is wrong, we might find ourselves headed in a completely wrong direction. It is true that there is a dangerous aspect to prayer, because inherent in it is the fueling of desire. If a prayer becomes a prayer of greed, there is a possibility that we will come under negative spiritual influences.

So pray with a calm mind and without attachment. It is important to pray along the following lines, "Please let my wish be realized at the appropriate time, if it is in accordance with the will of God."

4. The Universe Is Filled With Energy

When we think about prayer, we cannot ignore the perspective of the universe as filled with energy. Human beings tend to forget this. We often fall into states of loneliness, and feel as if we have been left behind in a desert or on the surface of the moon. Then we pray hard, believing there is no one there to help us.

In reality however, we are not alone. The universe is filled with wisdom and light, although we may not always be able to perceive this. It is overflowing with the energy of love. When we realize this, we will understand that we are surrounded by many who are ready to support us, and that the universe is filled with many thoughts to help us succeed.

If we consider the concept of success, for instance, the energy of the universe is actually filled with factors that bring success. At the heart of God are the concepts of prosperity and development. The concepts of wealth and abundance are found throughout the universe, and these thoughts are realized in various forms in many different places on this planet. People become successful as actors, statesmen, business people, doctors and writers, for example, and in many other professions. These successes are manifestations of the energy that is working to bring people wealth. There is no limit to God's love.

American economist and professor Lester Carl Thurow

(1938–) published a book on the idea of "zero sum." In economics, there is the idea of "zero sum," which means that if someone takes part of a pie, other people get that much less of it because the total amount of pie is fixed; it neither increases nor decreases. For instance, if someone cuts and eats part of an apple pie, the size of the pie is reduced by that much. If each person eats half of the pie, only two people can have some. If eight people share the pie, each of them can eat only an eighth. The sum total does not change; this is his concept of "zero sum."

This way of thinking is true of what happens on Earth. For example, in a company, if someone is promoted to the only available position, then you do not get it. Or if someone passes an entrance exam for the last place at a school, you will miss out. But this zero-sum type competition is not the only truth.

God's thoughts of success have nothing to do with the number of people who succeed. It is not His wish for only one person in a million or a billion to succeed, or that in a company the success of one person is sufficient. God intends to allow all those who have a certain level of ability to be successful. If a person's attitude and the effort they make is of a certain level, that person will definitely enter a flow of success and will experience success in many areas of his or her life.

If someone who is competent is unable to succeed in a particular company, that person might set up a new company on his or her own, or change jobs and accomplish something far greater. This is how things work, so you should not wish for easy success, like winning a lottery. You should not hold onto the idea of the zero sum, and believe that if one person is successful, others must necessarily fail. This kind of thinking excludes others and creates a self-centered world, which shuts out other people.

The universe is filled with energy that will make you happy. It is important to know how to bring this flow of energy to yourself, and this is connected to how to pray.

5. Methods of Prayer

Next, let us consider how to pray. Members of our organization who have taken refuge in the Three Jewels of Buddha, Dharma and Sangha are given the sutras, "Prayers I" and "Prayers II." These sutras include many prayers such as "Prayer to the Lord," "Prayer to Guardian and Guiding Spirits," "Buddha's Teaching: Sutra for Our Ancestors," and "Prayer for Recovery from Illness."

There are two kinds of prayers: prayers for realizing one's wishes, and prayers asking to be charged with energy. Prayers asking to be charged with energy are less dangerous to practice. You sit with a calm mind and pray to God, "Please give me infinite energy, infinite wisdom and infinite love." While you are praying, you visualize yourself receiving the light that is being sent down to you from the heavenly world.

Visualize, for example, God's infinite love flowing into you. When you feel that you have been filled with infinite love, next think about how you will radiate that energy out into the world. When you feel recharged through visualizing God's eternal power pouring into you, it is important to think about how you will live and your contribution to the world using this infinite power.

The safest prayer is asking to be charged with energy, so I recommend you use this. In fact, I often use this prayer myself. I work every day, and there are days when I feel tired or I am not in good shape. At these times, I always receive light from the high spirits. There are times when I am infused by the light of God directly, but usually I call on high spirits for help. Then the light pours into me, and I become filled with energy and am able to continue my work.

The high spirits will gladly fulfill this kind of prayer by pouring light into us. On the other hand, there are difficulties connected to prayers for realizing particular desires or success in a particular endeavor. I frequently pray to be charged with energy, and the high spirits help me quite a lot. However, I hardly ever pray for a specific vision to manifest because one path opens up after another before I have actually wished for it.

Another way to put this is: If your mind is focused in the right direction and you are making a daily effort, a path will open before you of its own accord, like an automatic door. It is the power of the high spirits that opens up the way. This is how things happen naturally, without having to wish too strongly for them.

The effort required of human beings living on Earth is to withstand the test of time, to wait patiently for a certain period of time. Yet you should not simply wait and do nothing; while waiting, you should do what you can and be ready to accept what is given when it is given. After you have received something, it is important that you then use it for the good of the world.

I would like you to remember that deep within, a prayer should contain a high ideal. The prayers of those who do not have high ideals will only go round and round vainly within the shell of the ego. I sincerely hope that when you pray, you have ideals that are pure and lofty.

Chapter Four

Shining Moments in Life

1. Abundance in Mother Nature

In this chapter, I would like to discuss the shining moments in life. To begin with, let us think about the vigor of Mother Nature. Summer is a remarkable time because during this season all life is at its most brilliant. If we go outside in summer, we will find that the sunlight is very strong, the leaves on the trees are deep green and shadows are darker than usual. At this time we feel the pulsing, luxuriant nature of life.

When we feel the breath of life in Mother Nature, we cannot help but think about the cycle of the seasons. Why did God create four seasons in one year? Why do we have winter, spring, summer and autumn? What is the meaning of living in this cycle of the seasons? Although we may live without ever paying attention to these sorts of things, at times we should consider their significance. When we stop and think carefully about this, we become aware that each season has its own significance.

As one of the four seasons created by God, what is the significance of summer? What are the ideas or themes of summer? What is summer intended to express? Here, I would like to point to the three main themes that seem to be inherent in summer.

The first is the quality of abundance. If we look at the colors of Mother Nature in each season, the greatest variety is to be seen in summer. By abundance I mean the vigor and strength that are the heart of summer. The hardiness of weeds and wild plants in particular often touches our hearts. The stems and leaves of these wild plants grow thick and powerful in the summer, and it is as if they will never stop growing. On seeing them, for some reason we become aware of the weakness and mediocrity of human beings, and the feebleness of the light humans give out.

Why do wild plants thrive so powerfully? From another perspective, we can see that God has granted these plants the power to thrive, plants which people rarely even know the names of. We should learn something from this. Although wild plants do not generally have beautiful flowers, they express vigor; they grow tenaciously, and this in itself is wonderful. We can well imagine that through their luxuriant growth, wild plants are expressing joy in living.

God does not only value appearance and outward beauty. While plants such as chrysanthemums and cherry trees bloom prettily, wild plants may not have a particularly beautiful appearance. However, they certainly constitute a unique feature of summer, and in their uniqueness lies the essence of abundance. Abundance is the power to grow and spread; it is the welling up of life force. This power to grow, spread and rise up is a sign of the prime of life. Even if we do not think of ourselves as being as beautiful as a dahlia, a chrysanthemum or cherry blossom, we can still appreciate and express our own vigor, just like wild plants.

The second quality of summer is that it makes us aware that decline will soon be creeping up on us. In their very prime, in the heyday of their lives, human beings feel the onset of decline. This is why when we hear cicadas singing incessantly in the trees in August, we associate their song with the winds of autumn that will start to blow before long.

Just before life fades, we often perceive its greatest beauty. It is like fruit at its most delicious, just before it goes bad. Similarly, summer, or the period when everything is abundant, contains within it signs of decline, and the beginning of the next stage. Simply because a light is destined to go out it seems to shine all the more brightly. So when we are in a period of development and prosperity, we need to be sensitive to and aware of the next stage—the decline—and take measures to cope with it. God teaches human beings this truth.

The third quality of summer is brightness. Summer is a season when we become aware of all the colors deepening brilliantly, and this vividness itself expresses a teaching. What constitutes this vividness? It is the brilliance of the light that living beings emit when they exert their inner power. Human beings tend to live each day out of force of habit, but there are times when we need to radiate a strong light. The brightness of summer teaches us that there are times when we must express the brilliance within.

The brightness of summer also teaches us the importance of having a positive influence on others. While abundance illustrates the wonder of growing and freely expressing life's full glory, brightness—or the intensity of light—signifies our influence or impact on others. So no matter what type of person you are, no matter what sort of society or culture you live in, in the prime of your life you should have the most influence on others.

2. Vigor

So far, I have singled out three qualities of summer; now I would like to analyze the power that is flowing at the heart of summer. If I were to summarize it in just one word, it would be "vigor." Why do all lives express such vigor in summer? Why is the force for growth so strong?

This vigor has two sources. The first is preparation; each plant and animal has been preparing through winter and spring to flourish and enjoy life in summer. Anticipating a period of growth, they have accumulated resources through this time. When accumulation exceeds a certain limit, it manifests in development and flourishing.

This is the result of a cumulative effect. For instance, when you collect a lot of data, after a certain point, that accumulation begins to exert a tremendous power. I often deepen my thoughts using this method. When I collect books, I do not limit myself to one particular topic. I choose and read books on many different subjects that arouse my interest. After some years, the information gradually constitutes a body of material that is valuable, out of which often flows a single theme that I compile and make into a book.

If you ask whether it is really wise to collect materials on the premise that you will later produce a book on a specific topic, the answer will not necessarily be "yes." If you continue to collect information on whatever catches your interest before you are clear about your final purpose, and if you constantly make an intellectual effort, when you reach a certain point, all these efforts will blossom as a result of the cumulative effect. There will be a time when an idea suddenly grows and blossoms in your mind.

In learning, I am always aware of the importance of preparation. You probably are, too. In studying the Truth, whether or not you have a specific purpose, you may find that in the beginning it is not easy to gain a clear understanding of what you are doing or where you are heading. However, if you continue studying, knowledge accumulates without you noticing, and when it has reached a certain point, it becomes the strength to convey the Truth to others, to influence other people and to open up the next stage for you.

All this happens as a result of a cumulative effect. If we closely observe the vigor in summer, we could say that it is the manifestation of what has been accumulating covertly through winter and spring.

The second source of vigor is environmental forces which play an important role. In summer, the environment is very dynamic. For example, hurricanes and typhoons blow up, bringing with them strong winds and rain; the sun's glare is sometimes relentless, and there is a greater difference between minimum and maximum temperatures, especially in desert or mountainous regions. With this dynamic change, the life force bursts forth.

Observing the vigor of summer, we notice the dynamism of the environment. During the seven or eight decades of our life, there are sudden changes in our environment; everyone undoubtedly experiences this kind of summer season several times in their life. When we notice our environment becoming more dynamic, we need to sense the coming changes and be aware that it is time for us to stand firm and take decisive action.

If you do not exert your power when you need to, you will not experience the vigor of summer. When you feel the environment becoming more dynamic, you need to express your life force. At these times, if you feel it is still winter and protect yourself, as if you were still under snow, your life will not truly open up before you. If you see the signs of change in your environment and feel it is time for you to take an active part, you should do your best to work positively. An inner accumulation of resources is indispensable as the basis for taking action.

3. The Law of Cycles

In each life, there are springs, summers, autumns and winters, which move in a different cycle from those of nature. For some people, a cycle will last three years, for others, five. There are also cycles of ten, twenty, even fifty years. The length of a cycle varies from person to person, and these cycles do not necessarily accord with the cycles of nature or the cycles observed by the laws of economics.

In fact, cycles vary according to the stature of a soul. Some souls require abrupt changes. Souls who are born with a great mission sometimes experience sudden changes in their environment, because their souls need to be forged and tempered with harsh experiences so that they will radiate light. These people may have to go through many hardships, one after another. For souls that have no need of such sudden changes and want peace rather than major shifts, the cycles are rather slower. These people lead lives where their environment changes little by little over ten or twenty years. Each soul requires different cycles.

Observing your own soul, what do you think the patterns are? Do you like sudden changes in life, like setting sail on a stormy night, or do you ask for a peaceful life, like the murmuring of a brook in spring? Here, too, differences in types of soul become clear. Those who like sailing on wild, stormy seas would probably not be satisfied with a life that did not have a lot of change. These souls have the potential for both great success and bitter failure. It is important to discover the cycles in your own life, to be able to observe the rises and falls, and ride through them successfully.

When living through the cycles in life, there are two important points you need to keep in mind. One is that when you are in a

period of decline, or a period of preparation, you need to focus
on accumulating inner resources. You should restrict the expendi-
ture of energy and focus instead on recharging and accumulating
inner resources. The other important point is that when the time
comes for you to be active and expend energy, it is important that
you apply yourself vigorously, without hesitating to use the inner
resources you have accumulated. It is also important at this time
that you start preparing for the next accumulation because as I
explained earlier, in times of development, the seeds of decline are
already present.

As long as you see your life plan from the perspective of cycles,
you will often be able to avoid major failure. On the other hand, if
you set your life plan in a linear not cyclical fashion, you will most
likely suffer setbacks when your situation changes, though there are
a few exceptions to this. Do not think that linear development in
just one direction is the only type of development. Development
does not just mean developing in a straight line. It is important to
know that there are spiral patterns of development, too. Although
you may appear to be in a decline for the time being, sometimes
this indicates a period of preparation for the next phase of development. Trying to create cycles that are linked to one another, like a
spiral staircase, is the right path to development.

4. A Beautiful Life

There are two types of questions you need to ask yourself when
living within the law of life cycles. One is: "Are you satisfied with
your life?" When you look back at the life you have lived, how does
it look to you? When you depart this world, at the age of sixty or
seventy or eighty, for instance, it is very important that you feel
satisfied with the beauty of your voyage, the beauty of the wake

that your boat has left behind as it moved forward. This does not necessarily mean you have to have achieved worldly success. What is important is that there is a certain beauty in the white waves created after your boat has passed.

By "beauty" I mean moments when your soul shines brilliantly. It is most important to have had at least one period in the sixty, seventy or eighty years of your life that you can show others with confidence. Perhaps you are proud of the time in your twenties when you made a great effort to study. Perhaps there was a time in your thirties when you worked hard to give something back to society, or perhaps you can point to a period of richness in later years.

Those who do not feel there is any period of their life that they can show others must have had very sad lives. Even if they experienced a lot of hardship, at some point they should also have experienced success. Even those who have known great success probably have some part of their lives that calls forth the sympathy of others. So it is important that each of us leaves beauty in the wake of the boat that is our soul.

The other question is: "Is there harmony in that beauty?" Here, harmony does not mean the harmony of the flow of your life, but the harmony that you create with those around you, and with your environment. When one ship sails forward beautifully, it is good, but the sight of a large fleet of ships advancing in formation is even more beautiful. If one ship advances straight ahead while another ship moves diagonally and another sails backward, the overall picture on the sea is not beautiful. When all the ships are moving forward in profound harmony, each leaving behind a beautiful wake, it is a truly magnificent sight.

So you need to check and see if there has been a period in

your life when you created your own beauty and at the same time created beauty in harmony with those around you. Were you able to create harmony with others, even when you were suffering? Were you able to live in harmony and beauty with others when you were successful and things were going well? It is important to consider these points.

5. Shining Moments in Your Life

I have discussed the theme of summer from several different angles. In a nutshell, the message of this chapter is: "What are the shining moments in your life? Explore them; pursue them." The season of summer poses this question for us. It also delivers a challenge: "Every year, Mother Nature creates a cycle and demonstrates brilliance in summer. Do human beings shine at least once a year? Are there shining moments in your life?"

Calm your mind and think deeply about this. The cycles of nature that God created contain this brilliance every year. If human beings, who have been given free will and who are allowed to be independent, do not experience any moments when they shine, it means that they are doing nothing more than living lazily.

Life without brilliance is a waste. Our ideal should be for shining moments to occur throughout our lives like flashing lights, and for this radiance not to be limited to ourselves but connected to the brightness of those around us, spreading through the country and out to the whole world.

Each of us has different potential and different abilities. We have each received a different education, been raised in a different environment, and of course, been brought up differently. However, no matter what the circumstances we find ourselves in, it is always possible for each of us to radiate the brightness of our soul. We can experience its shining.

I would like everyone to give out this brilliance. To find your own brilliance and confirm it for yourself is the first step to enlightenment; it is nothing less than the proof that you are living a life of Truth. I hope that you can become someone who has moments of shining, not just once a year but once a month, once a week or once a day. Only then can you say you are truly refining your soul.

Chapter Five

One Day As a Lifetime

1. Thoughts in Early Autumn

When the heat of summer comes to an end, we feel the winds of early autumn around us. How did you spend your summer? As autumn approaches and it becomes chilly, the efforts you made during summer will have some effect.

People who spent time developing their physical strength may gradually feel the motivation to start something new. Those who have been studying may want to study even more, as the result of a cumulative effect. Even those who spent summer lazily and did not do anything in particular may want a complete change of mood and make a new start. As I imagine the different thoughts people have, I also want to take the first steps toward autumn.

In autumn, when I sense the cold air in the mornings or feel the absence of friends and loved ones in the evenings, I notice that my thoughts often become philosophical and I come up with verses of poetry. Somehow this seems to be part of the mood of autumn. It is probably because the temperature is dropping, the trees and plants are preparing for winter after their burst of fullness in the summer, and crops are bearing fruit—all creating a distinctive mood.

In autumn, the words of literature often touch our hearts, probably because people become more sensitive at this time. Why do people believe that autumn is a good season for reading? Probably because it has long been regarded as the season for insights into life.

2. The Time of Harvest

I would like to contemplate harvest time. At Happy Science, what do we consider a "harvest"? What facts need to be confirmed for us to be able to say we have experienced a harvest? To be able to say this, we need to have fulfilled the following three conditions.

The first condition is that we are continuously exploring Right Mind, in order to live in accordance with God's will. We should not be satisfied just to explore Right Mind today and tomorrow, or when we first encounter the teachings of our organization. Rather, it is important that we continue pursuing this exploration for a year, two years, three years and on. When we can honestly say to ourselves that we have been exploring Right Mind every single day, then we can say we have experienced a "harvest."

At first, it is perhaps easy to agree to the practice of exploring Right Mind. However, as six months, a year, two years go by, people tend to forget their original resolution. They shut their eyes to their own shortcomings and let their desires begin to grow. This is why we always need to make sure that we go back to the start and return to Right Mind.

The practice of exploring Right Mind does not work like saving money. If you have savings, you can use them little by little, and they will last for some time. However, the effort of exploring Right Mind is limited to a single day, and the concept of savings does not apply. Right Mind is something that needs to be practiced in every moment. Therefore, it is very important to keep up a daily practice of exploring Right Mind.

A second prerequisite for experiencing a harvest is to feel

confident that we have reached a certain level in our study of the Truth. Three practices are outlined as activities of Happy Science: the exploration of the Truth, its study, and conveying the Truth to others. These three items should be practiced in this order.

First comes an individual exploration of the Truth. This means trying to understand what the Truth is for oneself, based on the practice of exploring Right Mind. As for the advanced level, this also means constantly trying to make new discoveries about the Truth in the process of searching and exploration.

Next comes study. This means getting rid of all preconceptions and trying to understand the teachings in the books of Truth in a correct, unprejudiced way. It also means making an unsparing effort to study, and reaching a certain level of achievement as the result of this accumulated effort. The importance of studying the Truth cannot be overemphasized; some people mistakenly compare it to studying at school, and take it too lightly. But studying the Truth while you are alive is extremely valuable.

There are many people in the world who do not yet know the Truth. When they return to the other world, these people will be shocked at the tremendous gap that exists between their worldly ways of thinking and knowledge of the Truth. Some of them will have to undergo spiritual discipline in the realm known as hell, but they are not entirely to blame; the reason they made mistakes during their lives on Earth is that unfortunately, they did not know the Truth.

Still, they should not hold others responsible for their own ignorance. They cannot blame the Ministry of Education for not having given them an opportunity to learn spiritual Truth at school. The reason they cannot defend themselves with this sort of excuse is that the seeds of the Truth existed in various forms when they were on Earth, but they did not take these teachings seriously, ignoring them, so they have to take responsibility for their lack of effort.

Even if people do not go to hell, many will be bewildered by the great gap between their own thinking while they were living on Earth and the Truth of the spirit world. After death, these people will go to the Posthumous Realm of the fourth dimension where they will wander confused for a long time. If they had acquired more knowledge of the Truth, they could have returned more quickly to the realms they originally came from, to continue their studies. However, since they did not study the Truth, their time on Earth could be the cause of delay in their spiritual evolution.

For this reason, I would like the movement for the study of the Truth to spread more widely, and usher in an age when everyone studies the Truth. This is why we should not regard the study of the Truth as being the same as studying at school. Expanding the movement for the study of the Truth is one way of conveying the Truth. This is one truly significant path to salvation.

The third condition for being able to say we have experienced a harvest is that once we have explored and studied the Truth, we convey it to others. How have you applied and made use of the Truth you have learned? After studying, did you simply store the knowledge away or were you able to use even a small portion of it to assist the development of friends and people you met in the course of your life? Have you been able to influence many of those you have met in a positive way? It is necessary to check on these things.

If you simply store up the Truth as a treasure for yourself, it will be fruitless. That is like stacking up crops in the fields after you have gathered them, and not putting them into a storehouse. This cannot be considered a real harvest. To be called "a harvest," the crop has to be stored properly so it can benefit others, which is its true purpose. Once you have studied the Truth, it is important to practice it, and then convey it to others, to guide and influence them in a positive way.

I have explained the three conditions for a harvest: the exploration of Right Mind and the Truth, its study, and conveying it to others. Only when you have reached the stage of conveying the Truth to others, and this can take many different forms, can you say that you have reaped a harvest for the first time.

3. One Day As a Lifetime

I have talked about the attitudes that those who seek the Truth at our organization need to have. Now I would like to use this opportunity to introduce a phrase that is at once ancient and modern: "Live one day as if it were a whole lifetime."

This phrase is based on the words of Jesus Christ in the Bible, "Therefore do not worry about tomorrow, for tomorrow will worry about itself. Each day has enough trouble of its own" (Matt. 6:34 NIV). The Japanese Christian leader Kanzo Uchimura (1861–1930) often quoted this. He said that to live each day as if it were a whole lifetime was the true way for Christians to live. This phrase is used not only by Christians but also by Buddhists and those belonging to other religions. The phrase implies that it is very important to live within the framework of a single day as if it were a whole lifetime.

The self-reflection that I have described on many occasions starts with thinking of each day as an entire lifetime. Some people may think, "A lifetime is a lifetime. I can reflect on my mistakes and make amends when I return to the other world." However, the mistakes and distortions created by the thoughts and actions of an entire lifetime cannot be corrected so easily.

It is like homework. It would be foolish to try to finish it all at once the day before it is due. This is why you do it little by little, so that it does not all pile up at the end. The same can be said of office work. You need to do it little by little, and complete a certain quota each day. An attitude of steadiness is important when working.

The same is true of self-reflection. True self-reflection is something that should be practiced each day, looking at that day as an entire lifetime, because human beings tend to forget things quickly. Usually, we can remember what has happened during the day until we go to bed. So, when you check on the thoughts you had during that day, you can remember the negative thoughts you entertained or the thoughts that were wrong. You can also reflect at length on your behavior that day, think about why you behaved in a particular way and consider whether there might have been a better way to react.

As the days pass, memories fade and no matter how hard you may try and reflect on them, they no longer feel as real. With the passage of time, you may think that mistakes have been forgiven and begin to forget them. However, the truth is that wrong thoughts and mistakes in everyday life will grow like cancer cells in your body. If you leave them unexamined, your body will be affected and eventually you will become spiritually ill. If you leave these "infected cells" in your mind, they will gradually spread, so it is necessary to test for these cells each day and cure them straightaway. I would like to emphasize strongly that for self-reflection, an attitude of living each day as if it were a whole lifetime is very important.

4. Dividing Your Worries Into Parts

The phrase "live each day as if it were a whole lifetime" has
another meaning; it can also be explained as a way of separating
out the chains of worry. It is true that we cannot control what is
too far in the future or what is already in the past, no matter how
much time we spend worrying about it. So dividing worries into
parts is actually a very important technique for attaining peace of
mind, because over eighty percent of the suffering of most people
comes from worrying too much about the future.

Often people worry about what might happen in a year's time,
in five years or ten years. This is an undeniable fact. People spend
more time worrying about the future, making vague predictions
about the following year or thinking vaguely about potential concerns in three years time rather than thinking what they can do in
the present.

In actual fact, there are not many worries we truly need to
concern ourselves with right now. When we look at the reality of
our worries, we find that most of them come from a tendency to
be over-anxious. In other words, most worries are unnecessary and
stem from a tendency to imagine misfortunes that might happen
in the future.

Suppose you are going to take an exam. It is understandable
that you may worry about whether or not you will pass. However,
if the exam is to be held in a year's time, there is no benefit in
worrying about passing now. In the present, what you can do is to
think about how to study more, and with greater efficiency, that
is to say, to improve both the quality and quantity of your study.
Worrying about whether or not you will be in good physical condition on the day you sit the exam is of no use whatsoever. Only

if you study, seeing each day as a battle, will a bright future open up for you.

The same is true of the past. There is no way you can change events you regret. If you constantly think about something that has happened in the past day after day, you are just regenerating the worry, and making it bigger. For example, if you are concerned about something rude you said to someone a week ago, if you want to live according to the framework "each day is a lifetime," the only thing you can do is to apologize directly to that person today. If you can do this, in that moment, you will be able to stop worrying. However, if you do not have the courage to apologize, you will have to worry continuously today, tomorrow and the day after about what you said a week ago.

In most cases, people who are considered "experts on life" are very good at separating out the chains of worry. For those who are able to make quick decisions about whether or not a problem can be solved right now by worrying about it, the burdens in life do not become so weighty. These people are able to live with a clear, unburdened attitude.

Let me take the example of removing snow from the roof of a house. If snow on a roof is wet and heavy, and is not removed for quite a period of time, it can build until it crushes the house beneath its weight. Given that the accumulated snow can crush a house, it is important to think about how to prevent this from happening.

Although in this case the snow weighs several tons, no special equipment is needed to remove something so heavy. People do not use bulldozers to bring the snow down from the roofs; they simply remove it little by little, using shovels. In spite of the fact that snow can build to a weight of several tons, even children can help to remove it using shovels. Eventually, the snow is completely removed from the roof.

Getting rid of worries is the same as the removing of snow from the roof. If you leave your worries for a long time they will become massive, but it is not so difficult to solve them little by little. The work of removing the snow is the equivalent of practicing self-reflection within the framework of a single day, and living each day as if it were a whole lifetime. It is extremely difficult to think about how to make a whole life shine at its brightest, but it is not so difficult to think about how to make each day shine brilliantly.

The same is true for the study of the Truth. You cannot read a lot of books all at once, so the steady effort of studying one book at a time is required. Think deeply about living each day as if it were an entire lifetime, using the metaphor of removing snow from a roof.

5. A New Life

I have focused on the theme "one day as a lifetime." This phrase can be used in a different way to mean "thinking of each day as the beginning of a new life." What is most frightening for human beings is not any outside enemy, not illness nor death. What is most to be feared is actually boredom in everyday life, feeling lazy, following the same routine day in, day out. This is the very thing that torments us as if we are slowly and insidiously suffocated by soft cotton. In the monotony of everyday life, we become unable to breathe fresh air and live freely. Most of us are in situations where we are slowly being suffocated. So we could say that the real cause of anxiety lies in day-to-day dullness.

If this is the case, what should we do? What do we need to do if we want to start afresh every morning with the feeling that each day is an entire lifetime? Every day we need to devise new ways of improving our lives. This is the first step to embarking on a new life.

Do not be content just to practice self-reflection, in the framework of a single day. You should see the day as the starting point for hope, regarding every morning as a new beginning, and thinking about what you need to discover or what you can create that day. Yesterday is gone, so think about what you can do today to make it fruitful, and what you would like to have harvested by this evening.

Every day, find new ways of improving your life. It will be a constant series of successful days for those who constantly try to devise something new. The difference between people who are ruled by day-to-day boredom and those who think of each morning as a new departure will eventually be huge.

What do you think of at the beginning of a day, a day that is equivalent to a lifetime? What will you think about and what will you try to do? How will you improve the way you live? How will you correct your attitude? What kind of perspective will you have on life? Think about these things once again. If your daily life does not change and you do not embark on a new life, it means that you have not really read my words. I ask each one of you to be ready to find your own answers to the questions, "What does it mean to begin a new life?" and "What represents a new day?"

Chapter Six

The Oneness of God and the Self

1. Experiencing the Presence of God

You can study a wide variety of the Truth through books of Happy Science. When you understand the Truth in the depths of your heart, you will experience new emotions; when you feel these you are experiencing the presence of God. It is very easy to say that you have experienced God, but the actual experience of this is not so simple. Your whole life reveals the true depth of your actual experience of God.

As for "enlightenment," perhaps you think of it as a faraway state, rather like a diamond you can only find if you dig deep for it. Actually enlightenment is the extent to which you truly experience and sense God. When you experience God, you are affected by His presence. If you are receptive to His influence, you feel a greater need to transform yourself to come closer to Him. So it is important that you have as many moments as possible when you truly experience God.

Even those people who are deeply impressed when they first read the words of the Truth, sometimes mistakenly begin to take them for granted as time goes on and see only their value for this world. I would like once again to remind these people that to encounter an extensive array of the Laws of Truth is an exceptional opportunity. It is truly a miracle that is now happening on this Earth.

If you no longer experience this encounter with words of the Truth as miraculous, it may be because you are not making a consistent effort to better yourself on a daily basis. Rather than passing each day aimlessly, it is important to continue daily to make new discoveries. Each time you encounter words of the Truth, have a positive attitude, and always try to discover something new. When you read a book of the Truth, rather than just reading the words without giving them much thought, study each idea carefully, sometimes by making notes for example, and engraving the words that embody light deep into your memory.

Unless you truly understand these teachings, the knowledge from them cannot become your own. When learning, you should never forget the words of Confucius, "By exploring the old, one comes to understand the new." This means that in the process of learning, you occasionally need to go over what you have learned previously and make sure that you have truly assimilated the vast store of knowledge. Even if you felt you understood the Truth when you first read it, as your inner self changes over the course of a year or two, you will make new discoveries. Then you will become keenly aware just how much magnificent Truth you have missed.

2. The Basis of Self-Reflection

The basis for self-reflection is the Truth. Without this basis, your reflections will only be superficial. People seem to have some misconceptions about self-reflection; they imagine that reflecting on the self involves looking back on the past from a remote setting, like a secluded mountain retreat. Yet true self-reflection is not like that of a criminal, sitting in a solitary cell contemplating past sins.

Many people seem to have the idea that self-reflection is

something passive. There is, of course, this aspect but self-reflection can also be proactive in that it is a way to refine and develop the self. Yet another way that people seem to view self-reflection is simply as a way of repenting past sins, or thoroughly examining past thoughts and deeds. These are essentially traditional inter-pretations of self-reflection that undoubtedly have some value. However, this level of reflection is no different from the practice of many Buddhist seekers in the past, and if you are satisfied with this, there is no point in learning reflection at Happy Science.

Inner contemplation is one method of self-reflection that is excellent for checking for mistakes in your thinking. However, if you want to master true self-reflection, you should not be satisfied with this level but advance courageously to active reflection. Of course it is necessary to clear away any clouds created in the past that cover the mind, but this is not enough. You also need to see reflection as a positive way of creating a brighter future.

Past failures serve as great lessons for the future, and at the same time, as indispensable springboards for future action. For this reason you do not need to be afraid of the process of trial and error. For those who acquire nourishment by learning from every experi-ence, and leap forward using their experiences as springboards, self-reflection becomes a great tool for directing your life in a positive and constructive way.

Some people may think that reflection is on past events, and that prayer deals with events of the future. Of course there is some truth in this, but I would like you to know that reflection can also be future oriented. Similarly, there are prayers to give thanks for past events as you look back on your life, and also prayers for con-fessing past sins. Self-reflection and prayer cannot really be divided, and we cannot say that reflection is always oriented to the past and prayer to the future. Neither can it be said that reflection is a passive approach whereas prayer is more active. There are similarities between self-reflection and prayer, as well as differences.

I would prefer to say that reflection typically places more importance on checking the inner self. It is a way of discovering areas where things have already gone wrong, and correcting them in a positive way for the future. In other words, reflection is the act of bringing yourself closer to your true nature as a child of God; in this respect, true prayer and self-reflection are very similar.

If I were to explain the difference between prayer and reflection, I would say that there are times when prayers are misguided because we are given so much freedom in the direction we send them. However, as long as prayer is turned in the right direction, the direction of becoming one with God, it is not very different from reflection. However, I can say that prayer is a relatively easy path while reflection is more arduous, requiring effort, and it is based on the spirit of self-help.

3. What Is a Thought Tape?

At Happy Science, we teach that there is a part of the human mind where all of a person's thoughts and deeds are recorded, as if on a tape recorder. This is called a "thought tape." Thought tapes can become covered by "dust" or "clouds" that arise from wrong thoughts and actions, and can hinder the light of God from shining through.

What is this thought tape and what is its purpose? The thought tape is very mysterious; it cannot be explained with the metaphor of a veil or a curtain. We can easily play back a high quality recording of beautiful music when we listen to a compact disc, and in a sense, the thought tape is similar to a compact disc. With spiritual eyes, we can detect this thought tape, perfectly placed in the region of the chest rather than the brain, and the nature of the thoughts and deeds that are being recorded are clearly visible.

This kind of recording mechanism is built into everyone; it is not used only for recording and saving but also in daily life for playing back memories. In other words, everyone is always playing back the "music" that has been saved on the CD in their own heart. On a single CD, there are many different kinds of music; each day people choose from the various types of music, depending on their mood and the situation they find themselves in.

The fact that everyone is playing their own music all the time means that on hearing the music, the angels in heaven instantly understand the kind of music a person usually plays. In fact, each tone of the music has a spiritual wavelength, signifying its spiritual level, and attracting what responds to that wavelength.

This is not a complex mechanism; it is based on a simple principle that is easy to understand with a worldly analogy. When you play a recording of certain music, people who love that music will naturally be attracted to it while those who do not like it will gradually drift away. People who love classical music, for example, will gather with others who share their love of it, and those who do not like it will not be interested.

I have described the thought tape in auditory terms. The thought tape is not a real object, but a kind of mechanism that keeps records in the heart area. If this thought tape is covered with clouds, it means the melody being recorded will not be harmonious. It is as if discordant notes have occurred in the middle of a performance of a piece of music, which otherwise would be as good as that of a professional musician. It can be likened to the snapping sound of a violin string, or a high-pitched note from the piano that suddenly breaks into the music, creating an uncomfortable effect.

Since the high spirits are expert at understanding "spiritual music," they are quite sensitive to anything that detracts from it. Just as professional musicians feel uneasy when there is poor piano-playing or singing, high spirits have difficulty attuning themselves to someone who is not in harmony with their wavelength. Although amateurs of "spiritual music" may not be disturbed by a few small mistakes, the high spirits are very sensitive to any disharmony. You need to be conscious of the high standards of the higher spirits.

4. The History of a Soul

I have just described the thought tape using the metaphor of a CD. This thought tape or CD of the spirit world not only plays the "music" of the present; it has a multilevel structure. Every thought and deed from this life is recorded on a single disc and on the reverse side is another disc that has recorded a person's thoughts and deeds in the heavenly world. Under this disc is another disc that has recorded a previous life on Earth, and beneath is a disc of the life before that, and so on. In this way, many discs are stacked in a small box in the heart.

To understand the ancient history of a soul, you need to select the old CDs and play them. By listening to the music that recorded in past incarnations, you can know what kind of melody you were playing each lifetime. Whether a person likes it or not, every thought and deed in a human life is recorded, and in this way the history of a soul becomes more substantial.

At Happy Science, we also teach the theory of brother and sister souls, and of core and branch spirits. A human soul is not just an individual being but is part of a soul group together with several other entities that remain in the spirit world. This can be translated into worldly terms by saying that there are many different CDs of past reincarnations in a soul, and if we play the music back, details of previous lives will become clear in the form of specific music.

The relatively recent history of a soul, of the past few hundred or thousand years for example, is recorded so vividly that it can be reproduced as if that person were living in the present. On the other hand, if you are dealing with records made ten thousand, a hundred thousand or a million years ago, those records cannot be reproduced as if the life were being lived right now. Rather, the life appears as just one book in a vast library of records.

I see the past lives of high spirits, listen to them and convey their words. However, the spirits who address me as individual human souls are mostly those who have lived in the last ten thousand or at most twenty thousand years. Those who lived before that time no longer have an individual form; the ancient soul memories become like a history book that is stored in a library. In this way, every time you live a new life, a new CD is produced and the old CDs are moved to the area where memories are stored.

5. The Oneness of God and the Self

I have talked of experiencing the presence of God, and spoken about self-reflection in relation to the thought tape and the history of the soul. Lastly, I would like to introduce yet another point of view. Be it self-reflection, meditation or prayer, what is most important is how deeply you experience oneness with God. You need not be too concerned about the method. What I am constantly trying to address in my books and lectures is how to actually experience your oneness with God. I would like your goal to be to reach the state where you are completely united with God.

This is the same as the idea of "the oneness of Brahma and atman" in ancient India. The word "Brahma" is a general term signifying Buddha, God and high spirits. Before Shakyamuni's birth, the idea was handed down that Brahma and the self were one and the same, although they appeared to be different and separate. Later Shakyamuni also taught this idea more lucidly.

Although I am using a different language, my intention is to express the same idea. I am trying to clarify the true nature of God, His many different aspects and His various manifestations, as well as ideal attitudes for human beings. What I am trying to say is this: Although each of you has a different character, within these differences there is a way for everyone to attune to God. Discover the way and go forward bravely. Walk straight on the path, and you will find true enlightenment.

Those who have succeeded in attaining a state of oneness with God and maintaining this state for long periods during the day, or those who were able to experience the oneness of God and the self for long periods during their lifetime will eventually reach a high level of development and become high spirits when they return to the spirit world. I would like you to savor the state of oneness with God at least once in this life, if possible two or three times, or even more. To this end, I will continue to write unceasingly.

Chapter Seven

The Prelude to a New Era

1. Anticipating a New Era

The number of the Laws of Truth that I teach has increased tremendously. Now I am considering how best to compile this ever-expanding number of Laws to present them in a more comprehensible way. While I am working on this, the approach of the coming era constantly occupies my thoughts; I feel I must not lose sight of it for even a moment.

The main purpose of the activities of Happy Science is to create a great wave to launch the new era. For this reason, the Laws that I teach and the Truth we are conveying need to be imbued with a sense of the coming era.

As I close my eyes and calm my mind, there are at least three things I anticipate will happen in the new age. The first is things that are generally accepted and highly valued by society now will completely collapse in times to come. This change will be obvious enough for everyone to see clearly and feel it happen. It may be an experience that will give us greater self-confidence.

I feel enormous energy in what is about to emerge. Just like a huge whale that comes to the surface of the ocean from the depths of the sea, showing its fins and spouting water, values that have until now been hidden will come to the fore in the new era. Anticipation of this is growing stronger day by day.

The second thing I anticipate happening is that people will

experience the presence of God very near. I can see this even with my eyes closed and I can hear it even with my ears covered; it echoes in my heart. We cannot deny that God is close to humankind. We can feel Him so close. We can see God before us, and hear His voice, strongly encouraging us. There is no better time than now to experience the presence of God. The time will come when God appears before humankind, a time known only in legend and in the old scriptures.

The third thing I anticipate is that we will feel the whole universe is closer to us. I have the wonderful expectation that the great universe, which up to now has been shrouded in mystery, will become more known and comprehensible to humankind.

My anticipation of these three things swells and fills my heart. Day by day, I feel we are advancing in the direction I have described, and I am sure that many who gather at Happy Science also feel the approach of a new era. I believe that I am not the only one feeling dizzy with anticipation of current values being overturned, the presence of God being experienced by everyone, and the cosmos becoming known more closely.

2. The Turning Point of Our Era

Humankind is now standing at the turning point of an era. It will bring great achievements, but at the same time it will be accompanied by a large scale collapse of many of the present forms. On an international level, what has had great influence in the world will gradually lose its power, and what has been considered unimportant will begin to assume importance. Renewal will also take place at a national level.

At this time, we need to think about the following two issues. The first is how to harvest the abundance of what humankind has produced thus far. This means harvesting what humankind has created up to this point of civilization, and leaving it as a legacy for future generations.

The second important issue is preparing for the challenges that are to come. Human beings will face many important challenges to overcome for some years, and we have to be strong enough to endure for a certain time. Not just a handful but many countries will experience different kinds of hardship and confusion.

At such times, you need to think about how to maintain peace of mind, the unshakable mind, and how to live in accordance with the will of God. It is also important to know how to be content. People tend to overestimate their abilities. They feel dissatisfied with their current situation and imagine they deserve a better life or that they should be valued more highly. It is a human tendency to desire better opportunities, a higher income, and greater recognition from others.

However, you need to think about how you would feel if the stage you are now standing on were to crumble and disappear. People often quarrel with their spouse or partner about trifling matters, and couples feel dissatisfied with each other. But they should give more thought to the hard times to come, and stop letting petty thoughts disturb their peace of mind.

If you complain a lot about your income, your environment, your work or your status, you need to be aware that humankind will face much harder times. In times of hardship, if your mind is disturbed by trifling concerns, you will certainly not be able to survive major difficulties. Instead, you need to think about how to overcome the hardships that confront the whole of humanity.

It is important to accumulate the strength little by little to prepare for such times. One requirement is to accumulate the strength not to be affected by any kind of suffering, difficulty or misfortune. The other is to accumulate a knowledge of the Laws of Truth, and build within a foundation of these, so that no matter what happens, you are able to hold on to the Truth.

3. A New Kind of Enlightenment

What kind of challenges have you been given, as you stand on the turning point of an age? Now that you stand at this point, you need to find a new kind of wisdom.

Those who seek the Truth should not be satisfied just to study the teachings of traditional Buddhism, which are some two thousand five hundred years old, or the teachings of Christianity from two thousand years ago. It is not enough just to revive those old teachings. Instead, discover a new wisdom, and open up a path to a new kind of enlightenment. Unless you do this, there is no point in being alive at this time, and there is no way of explaining why you are living now.

What do you think this new enlightenment is? This era will eventually pass. Try and look back at your present self from one thousand or two thousand years into the future. From that standpoint, what sort of wisdom could you say that you were acquiring in the present?

New enlightenment should not just be a revival of Buddhism. You need new teachings and a new philosophy. There is an indispensable element that should be a part of these new teachings and the new enlightenment. This is the principle of action. I have been telling you how important it is to study the Truth, but now you have come to a new turning point, you should not be content just to study. What you have studied needs to be assimilated, so that it becomes the basis for your own set of new principles for action.

It must forge new standards for behavior and new principles to act upon. The new kind of enlightenment must be backed up by practical application. It must be a wisdom that enables you to live through the present age, to fight and overcome the problems that you are actually facing.

For those of you who are studying to attain happiness, your challenge must be to practice what you have learned. First, explore happiness and discover methods of attaining it. Do not leave it at abstract ideas or a series of theoretical teachings. Put what you have learned into practice in your daily life. Like Zen koans to contemplate in Buddhism, contemplate concrete methods for creating a life of happiness every day. The Laws of Truth must not remain abstract knowledge, they must be brought down to a practical level.

I would like to emphasize that assimilating knowledge of the Truth is what is most important. You need to digest the knowledge of the Truth, bring it down to the practical level, and make sure that what you have learned is being put into practice in your everyday life. Unless you do this, there is no point in studying the Truth. If you are studying now, what you have studied must be expressed in your actions in daily life. This is something that I would particularly like you to bear in mind.

4. The Bells of Hope Are Ringing

Although we are heading into hard times and those who live in this era have a big challenge ahead, I have no intention of emphasizing only the darker side of what lies before us. Living in times like these means that we are also living in times of hope, when we can achieve great things. I can hear and see the bells of hope ringing.

I would like you to think deeply about the significance of the fact that you are living in an age of such magnificent blessings, an age when miracles are becoming an everyday event. I would also like you to check and see that you are not simply drifting, carried along on the currents of everyday habits, and make sure that you are not content to achieve only easy goals each day.

In ancient Egypt, Moses and Aaron went to Pharaoh and showed a miracle. However, although Pharaoh witnessed the miracle of Aaron's staff changing into a snake, he could not hold on to his belief in what he had seen for even a day (Ex. 7:10). Check and see whether you have become like Pharaoh. It is true that one of the objectives of Happy Science is to make miracles an everyday occurrence. However, even after this has been accomplished, you should not lose your capacity to believe in miracles, nor start taking them for granted.

Now is the prelude to the approach of the era of God, and numerous Laws of Truth are being taught. If anyone is reading these Laws as if they were reading fairy tales or editorials, I would like them to show their respect by reading them once more with an open mind. Think again about the value of encountering these Laws at this point in time.

What would people from one thousand or two thousand years in the future think, if they could see you living in this era? The answer to this shows you that you are living now in an age of miracles. There is no doubt that people one or two thousand years from now would wish that they had been able to be here. Never forget that you are living at a remarkable time, when there is an abundance of happiness and hope. It is a time when God is present. He is standing right there, knocking on your door. I would like you to reorient your mind to the solemn fact that you are living in a time of miracles.

Calm your mind and listen carefully. You will hear the bells of hope ringing. No doubt you can hear a beautiful melody. If you have ears, you will surely hear it; if you have eyes, you will surely see the bells ringing. I hope everyone will awaken to this fact.

5. The Distant Future

Our goal is not just to live in the present; our eyes should also be fixed on a far distant world, on times far into the future. Our daily efforts should be dedicated to creating a legacy for human beings for the future.

Do not be satisfied with the same old routine, without any joy or happiness. It is not enough just to bring salvation to the people of this time and happiness to the society of today. It is also important to be enthusiastic and determined to bring happiness to those who will live in the future as well. Only with this enthusiasm does living in this age of hope and blessings have great significance.

Become a new Angel of Light, every one of you, like one of the ten great disciples of Buddha, or the twelve disciples of Jesus Christ. Although the future lies far ahead, you need to advance toward it. This is the challenge, a sacred task blessed by the Light. Free yourself from the passivity of daily life, move beyond the world of business, and break down old, fixed ideas. It is my sincere hope that more and more people will advance courageously, their eyes fixed on the far future.

Chapter Eight

Love, Light and Compassion

1. Talking About Dreams

Everyone has dreams. Dreams are not only the visions that come to us when we sleep. In real life, human beings can easily lose their way but even at these times they can still have dreams.

Whenever December comes round, I remember the story called *The Little Match Girl,* by Hans Christian Andersen. A little girl from a poor family is ordered to go out and sell matches in the snow one cold New Year's Eve. Hardly anyone buys her matches, and she finally succumbs to the icy cold. Before she dies, she strikes the unsold matches and wonderful scenes appear, such as a Christmas tree and a kind grandmother. Perhaps you have read this story at some time.

When I think and talk of dreams, I cannot help remembering this tale. Dreams are so similar to the flames of this little girl's matches on a snowy night. Although the light from them is small, and flickers in the cold, it is a sure light that warms one for a moment. Then it goes out. I often compare life to a series of bright dreams; when one dream is extinguished, you want another dream. Then you light another match and see the next bright scene.

My job is to make a lot of "matches," like the ones the little match girl lit. Every day, I make many boxes of matches, one after another. Then I imagine people taking these matches and lighting them to warm their hands or to look around; perhaps the tiny flames throw light onto their faces or onto the snow around them.

They are only small flames, and they can give out only a little warmth. But no matter how faint the light, as long as they offer you some hope, matchmaking is a job I very much enjoy. I am a matchmaker, the president of a match-manufacturing company, so to speak, and I would like to continue making the matches that give rise to dreams. I wish very strongly to deliver bright light, heat and human warmth to every single person.

2. Love Blows Like the Wind

I very much like the word "love" and I have talked about it on numerous occasions. Although I have given discourses on various Laws and teachings, if I were asked to choose just one aspect to focus on, without a moment's hesitation I would choose the teachings of love. It is also because of love that I was born into this world, to share my life with you, and give discourses on the Laws. God is love, and I want to share this love with everyone.

Here it seems that my role is suddenly changing from that of president of a match manufacturer to Santa Claus. Santa Claus symbolizes exactly what I want to be. Every night, with a sack full of many different kinds of presents, I would like to clamber up onto the roof of each house, climb down the chimney, out through the fireplace and into the living room, find the empty stockings and fill them up with presents.

The problem would always be the size of my sack. No matter how big it was, it would not be big enough to hold all the presents I want to bring. When I think of the number of children in the world waiting for my presents, I feel that I need a much bigger sack. But Santa Claus cannot move if his sack is too big. He cannot get down narrow chimneys; so unfortunately, he has to carry a sack that is the right proportions for his body.

Can you see what I am trying to say with this metaphor? There are billions of people all over the world waiting to receive God's love. Now that I have been given the opportunity to live in this world, I want to deliver gifts from God to as many people as possible. I would like to go around putting them into the Christmas stockings of every single person. However, the number of presents that will fit into a sack is limited. Although I wish to give love without any limits, I have no means of doing so. This is this Santa's greatest regret.

Sometimes I feel like giving up on being like Santa Claus and instead become like the wind. I imagine how wonderful it would be if love could be passed on, not like the boxes of presents that Santa Claus gives, but like a wind blowing. If only I could be like the wind, expressing the power of love that blows from nowhere and blows to nowhere! A wind named Ryuho Okawa or Happy Science that originates in one corner of the globe and blows silently throughout the world, so pure and transparent that people would feel it only when it touched them. I would like to be a wind such as this, and I would like our organization to be such a wind.

Just like the wind, I want to rise out of nowhere and blow to nowhere. I would like to be a pure, selfless wind that arises and blows from here to there. I would like to be a wind that gives warmth in winter, a warm draft of air that blows through people's hearts as they wrap scarves around their necks and turn up the collars of their overcoats. I wish deeply that my love were boundless and unlimited, like the wind.

3. The Shimmering of Light

At other times, I wish I could be like light, not glaring or scorching, nor faint like the light that escapes through gaps in the clouds. The light that I am talking of is the soft, warm light you see in spring.

When the season is turning to winter, there are sometimes days when a warm, bright light shines on us, like the light of spring. On days like this, animals sometimes stir unexpectedly in hibernation and flowers start to bloom once again, drawn by this warm light and mistaking the warmth for the coming of spring. This is the kind of light I would like to be and transmit to every one of you. It is not just light, but a sparkling light. I wish to be like the clear, white brightness, the light of day that shines into every corner.

I love the way that light scatters on the surface of rivers, reflecting hundreds of small shimmering lights. I love seeing animals basking happily in the sun, or babies sleeping in soft warm sunlight, their mothers talking softly to them. I love seeing people exposing their backs to the sun, relaxing for a moment on a park bench, or watching the surface of a lake.

The showering of light seems to shower happiness with it. I wish I could be a warm, relaxing light, neither too powerful nor too faint for human eyes, creating a sparkling shower. Perhaps you can understand what I mean. This is my wish and I am sure you, too, would like to be this sort of light.

No matter where you are, you can give out light, like a warm spring day. So radiate your light, flashing here and there. Whenever you meet others, express a warm, benevolent light with your eyes. Try to understand the joys and sorrows of others as if they were your own, share your feelings with one another, and together spread happiness. I hope you will cultivate a compassionate heart.

4. Always Be Compassionate

My aspiration never changes; it is always to be compassionate. Sometimes you have to find the courage to speak resolutely, to make forceful decisions or take decisive action. However, beneath such actions there should always be a stream of kindness. Strong words and courageous actions are sometimes necessary if you want to lead as many people as possible to happiness. Because you are trying to be compassionate, you feel the need to be even stronger and more courageous.

What I am saying is not difficult. I would simply like you to be compassionate always. Even when you are in the midst of a busy work schedule or domestic difficulties, I would like you to remind yourself of the words: "Always be compassionate." When people lead satisfying lives, for instance when they are affluent or praised, they tend to take things for granted. So, every so often, they need to check and make sure they are not becoming arrogant or too hard on others.

Always be compassionate. No matter how kind you try to be, you can never be too kind. No matter how hard you try to live compassionately, you can never be compassionate enough. Each one of you who reads this message will leave this world one day. It may be in a few years or in a few decades time, but everyone will eventually leave this world. Can you imagine how you will feel when it actually happens? It will be as if you are leaving the Earth and becoming a star in the sky. It feels as if you are distancing yourself far from this world and becoming one of the stars out in space.

As you leave the Earth and fly hundreds or thousands of feet up into the sky, you will start to see the Earth as a tiny ball. Memories of the playground you ran around when you were small, your home and your friends, will become ever so distant and tiny.

The woods, the rivers, the mountains and what was once so familiar will become hazy. Then you will feel regret, and wish you had
been kinder to many more people. This moment will come, without fail, to everyone. At that time you will wish you had spoken
more kind words, and had been more loving to all those who are
dear to you. By repeatedly reminding yourself to be compassionate,
you are actually reminding yourself of the moment of departure
from this world.

Every single person dwells in their mother's womb, and is born
into this world to live for a number of decades. During this time,
people accumulate many different experiences. At some time in
the future, everyone will leave this world and return to the other
world. Life on Earth is a brief flash. It is like a fragment of memory
or a fairy tale, like a school trip or school days spent happily. All of
you are living just a brief moment in this world.

If this is so, why do you act so stubbornly, why do you want
to be so hard on yourself and others? If you have to leave this
world one day, why not fill it with warmth and sweet memories?
If you want others to be kind to you, why are you not kind to
them? Every moment you have ever felt happy is a moment when
someone else has been kind to you. Likewise, you should always
be compassionate to others. Just as you wish that others would be
compassionate to you, so you should always treat others in this way,
and live kindly.

Do you understand what I am trying to say? It is true that
sometimes too much kindness can have a negative outcome. Too
much kindness can sometimes spoil people. However, the world
is just about balanced out when people are a touch too kind. To
get rid of the harshness of this world, like dry winds that blow, a
little bit of too much kindness is just about right. Otherwise, how

can this society be transformed into something wonderful? I hope everyone will rediscover the lost value of compassion and take it back into their own hands as soon as possible.

5. What Is Human Happiness?

I have discussed love, light and compassion. Now, I would like to move on to human happiness. On different occasions I have looked at happiness from various angles and I have no intention of repeating what I said yet again. The only thing I would like to say here is that happiness is born of human relationships.

If you were the only being in this world, you would have no chance of experiencing happiness. If there was no one around, perhaps you would not experience unhappiness but you would certainly never have the chance to experience happiness. If you were living on a small South Pacific island all by yourself, you would hardly ever feel happy.

Human beings feel happiness and pleasure because there are other people to talk to, hold hands with, to love, work, live and learn with. Do not feel that you are isolated. Why not feel joyous at the fact that you have been given an individual life as a part of this vast world.

Would you feel happy if you were like a giant cedar tree, standing alone? There may be times when you feel sad or lonely because you are one tiny individual in an enormous crowd. However, it is actually because you are all tiny individuals that you are able to unite with others and share your life with them.

Human happiness has its origins in the fact that we are all individuals and at the same time, we are part of a crowd. Happiness arises between people. Looking at happiness in this way, how similar it is to love! Love also exists between people. How similar happiness and love are! Happiness is actually born of love. I am convinced of this.

Our solar system is part of the great universe and the Earth is only one of its planets. It is an amazing fact that more than six billion people share life on this Earth simultaneously. How remarkable this is! We are able to share our lives with so many other people. We can love many of those who are living at the same time as us. We can do things to make them more joyful. I would like you to think about how wonderful it is to be living in this sort of a world.

If you have relationships that are filled with love, you will not want anything else. You need to consider afresh how happy you would feel if you had these kinds of relationships. Think about what true happiness really is, bearing in mind that this world is a place that we will all leave behind one day. True happiness exists in love, in light and in compassion.

I have a dream of leading as many people as possible to happiness and giving love to as many people as I can. I always have this dream and it is my sincere hope that more people will walk with me and share my dream.

Love blows like the wind. Love is also like light that glitters brilliantly, showering happiness on all. Love exists in compassion. When you truly understand that this is the nature of love, and when you savor and nurture it for yourself, your happiness will expand limitlessly. So, let us bring happiness to many. Let us become happy ourselves and make others around us happy as well. I would like all of you to spread happiness, with the word "love" as your pledge.

Postscript

With infinite purity of heart, I have attempted to put into words the teaching of love. It is the most important teaching for every human being. Love is what we most aspire to. Love is our ideal; it is our heartfelt desire to soar without limits.

I sincerely hope that the Earth will be filled with people who are overflowing with compassion. With this hope, I have compiled one book. If you can understand this wish of mine, which is like a prayer, it will be the greatest happiness for me.

Ryuho Okawa
Founder and CEO
Happy Science Group
August 2001

About the Author

Ryuho Okawa, founder of Happy Science, Kofuku-no-Kagaku in Japan, has devoted his life to the exploration of the Truth and ways to happiness.

He was born in 1956 in Tokushima, Japan. He graduated from the University of Tokyo. In March 1981, he received his higher calling and awakened to the hidden part of his consciousness, El Cantare. After working at a major Tokyo-based trading house and studying international finance at the Graduate Center of the City University of New York, he established Happy Science in 1986.

Since then, he has been designing spiritual workshops for people from all walks of life, from teenagers to business executives. He is known for his wisdom, compassion and commitment to educating people to think and act in spiritual and religious ways.

He is a best-selling author of 100 million books sold worldwide, and has published titles such as *The Laws of the Sun*, *The Golden Laws*, *The Laws of Eternity*, *The Science of Happiness*, and *The Essence of Buddha*. He has also produced successful feature-length films (including animations) based on his works.

The members of Happy Science follow the path he teaches, ministering to people who need help by sharing his teachings.

Lantern Books by Ryuho Okawa

The Laws of the Sun: *Discover the Origin of Your Soul*
978-1-93005-162-1

The Golden Laws: *History through the Eyes of the Eternal Buddha*
978-1-59056-241-3

The Laws of Eternity: *Unfolding the Secrets of the Multidimensional Universe*
1-930051-63-8

The Starting Point of Happiness:
A Practical and Intuitive Guide to Discovering Love, Wisdom, and Faith
978-1-59056-312-0

Love, Nurture, and Forgive: *A Handbook to Add a New Richness to Your Life*
1-930051-78-6

An Unshakable Mind: *How to Overcome Life's Difficulties*
1-930051-77-8

The Origin of Love: *On the Beauty of Compassion*
978-1-59056-313-7

Invincible Thinking: *There Is No Such Thing As Defeat*
1-59056-051-5

Guideposts to Happiness: *Prescriptions for a Wonderful Life*
978-1-59056-314-4

The Philosophy of Progress: *Higher Thinking for Developing Infinite Prosperity*
1-59056-057-4

The Laws of Happiness: *Four Principles for a Successful Life*
978-1-59056-240-6

Ten Principles of Universal Wisdom:
The Truth of Happiness, Enlightenment, and the Creation of an Ideal World
1-59056-094-9

Tips to Find Happiness:
Creating a Harmonious Home for You, Your Spouse, and Your Children
978-1-59056-315-1

Order at www.lanternbooks.com

What is Happy Science?

Happy Science is an organization of people who aim to cultivate their souls and deepen their love and wisdom through learning and practicing the teachings (the Truth) of Ryuho Okawa. Happy Science spreads the light of Truth, with the aim of creating an ideal world on Earth.

Members learn the Truth through books, lectures, and seminars to acquire knowledge of a spiritual view of life and the world. They also practice meditation and self-reflection daily, based on the Truth they have learned. This is the way to develop a deeper understanding of life and build characters worthy of being leaders in society who can contribute to the development of the world.

Events and Seminars

There are regular events and seminars held at your local temple. These include practicing meditation, watching video lectures, study group sessions, seminars and book events. All these offer a great opportunity to meet like-minded friends on the same path to happiness and for further soul development. By being an active participant at your local temples you will be able to:

- Know the purpose and meaning of life
- Know the true meaning of love and create better relationships
- Learn how to meditate to achieve serenity of mind
- Learn how to overcome life's challenges

...and much more

International Seminars

International seminars are held in Japan each year where members have a chance to deepen their enlightenment and meet friends from all over the world who are studying Happy Science's teachings.

Happy Science Monthly Publications

Happy Science has been publishing monthly magazines for English readers around the world since 1994. Each issue contains Master Okawa's latest lectures, words of wisdom, stories of remarkable life-changing experiences, up-to-date news from around the globe, in-depth explanations of the different aspects of Happy Science, movie and book reviews, and much more to guide readers to a happier life.

Hundreds of interesting back-issues of our monthly publications are available at your nearest temple.

You can pick up the latest issue from your nearest temple or subscribe to have them delivered *(please contact your nearest temple from the contacts page)*. Happy Science Monthly is available in many other languages too, including Portuguese, Spanish, French, German, Chinese, and Korean.

Our Welcome e-Booklet

You can read our Happy Science Welcome Introductory Booklet and find out the basics of Happy Science, testimonies from members and even register with us:

http://content.yudu.com/Library/A1e44v/HappyScienceIntro

If you have any questions, please email us at:
inquiry@happy-science.org

Contacts

Find more information about Happy Science by visiting the websites below

Global Website
www.happy-science.org

Japan
www.kofuku-no-kagaku.or.jp/en
Tokyo
1-6-7 Togoshi, Shinagawa,
Tokyo, 142-0041 Japan
Tel: 81-3-6384-5770
Fax: 81-3-6384-5776
tokyo@happy-science.org

United States of America
New York
www.happyscience-ny.org
79 Franklin Street,
New York, NY 10013, U.S.A.
Tel: 1-212-343-7972
Fax: 1-212-343-7973
ny@happy-science.org

Los Angeles
www.happyscience-la.org
1590 E. Del Mar Blvd.,
Pasadena, CA 91106, U.S.A.
Tel: 1-626-395-7775
Fax: 1-626-395-7776
la@happy-science.org

San Francisco
www.happyscience-sf.org
525 Clinton St.,
Redwood City,
CA 94062, U.S.A
Tel: 1-650-363-2777
Fax: same
sf@happy-science.org

New York East
nyeast@happy-science.org

New Jersey
nj@happy-science.org

Florida
www.happyscience-fl.org
florida@happy-science.org

Chicago
chicago@happy-science.org

San Diego
sandiego@happy-science.org

Atlanta
atlanta@happy-science.org

Hawaii
www.happyscience-hi.org
hi@happy-science.org

Kauai
kauai-hi@happy-science.org

Canada
Toronto
www.happy-science.ca
toronto@happy-science.org

Vancouver
vancouver@happy-science.org

Europe
London
www.happyscience-eu.org
3 Margaret Street, London
W1W 8RE, United Kingdom
Tel: 44-20-7323-9255
Fax: 44-20-7323-9344
eu@happy-science.org

Oceania
Sydney
www.happyscience.org.au
sydney@happy-science.org

East Sydney
bondi@happy-science.org

Melbourne
melbourne@happy-science.org

New Zealand
newzealand@happy-science.org

To find more Happy Science
locations worldwide, go to
www.happy-science.org/en/
contact-us

Want to Know More?

Thank you for choosing this book. If you would like to receive further information about titles by Ryuho Okawa, please send the following information either by fax, post or e-mail to your nearest Happy Science Branch.

1. Title Purchased

_____

2. Please let us know your impression of this book.

_____

_____

3. Are you interested in receiving a catalog of Ryuho Okawa's books?
    Yes ❑   No ❑
4. Are you interested in receiving Happy Science Monthly?
    Yes ❑   No ❑

Name : Mr / Mrs / Ms / Miss: _____
Addres : _____

_____

Phone: _____
Email: _____

Thank you for your interest in Lantern Books.